A Window in Da' Hood

A Message to Animal Activists

Eldon Brown

Table of Contents

Dedication

I dedicate this book to my loving wife, Mrs. Katie Liz Brown. For standing by me through so many trials & tribulations and standing strong. For believing in me when I lost faith in myself. For telling me over and over again that I am more than a brutish person, when everyone we know only wanted to use me for my fighting ability. For loving me unconditionally, regardless of all my shortcomings.

Love is an emotion of total wonder. I cannot explain the love that I possess for my wife. My vocabulary is absolutely too limited. It is a feeling that is even incomprehensible to me. So, the best that I can do is say: Baby you are the quintessence of my soul. I manifest to you, that I define my manhood based upon my ability to make you happy. You give meaning to all in life that has value, because without you in my life, nothing will have value. I thank you for your love, beauty, strength, and wisdom. I thank you mostly, for giving me YOU.

I LOVE YOU BABY

Your Husband & Life Mate --Eldon

Introduction

My wife and I had the pleasure to attend the 2010 national animal rights convention in Alexandria, Virginia in 2010. On the first day there, we bumped into Dr. Jerry Vlasak and his lovely wife, Mrs. Pamelyn Ferdin, both of whom I've had the pleasure of meeting at a previous convention, in Portland Oregon in 2009. After introducing my Queen to my to friends, they invited us to get together with their friends later that night for some good conversation, and vegan beer (which I have to say was quite good).

We agreed, and after getting settled we went down to enjoy the company of our new friends. During our time with them that night, we had met some good and very memorable people. We ended up having a very intense discussion, which eventually led up to the question of: "How come we don't see that many minorities in the struggle for animal rights, and animal liberation?"

Katie, (my Queen), attempted to explain that most minorities aren't even familiar with animal rights. She continued, by explaining that animal activists don't go into the inner cities to enlighten minorities about animal activism; and secondly, we are so bombarded with a wide diversity of issues that the struggle for animal rights would seem bogus to us.

The next day, I continued this conversation with Dr. Vlasak, and he asked me "Why don't you write about it?" For the first time since I could remember, I was at a loss for words. I've never thought about writing on such a topic, but it seemed like an enjoyable challenge. Later that evening, I spoke to my Queen about it, and she felt that it was an excellent idea because that question was asked to us so many times. So, it's definitely time to answer this question.

Therefore, in this small book, "A Window in Da' Hood- A Message to Animal Activists," I will do my best to explain why there aren't many minorities in the struggle for Animal Rights, and Animal Liberation. However, let me also say that when I speak of minorities, I'm basically speaking of African American (Blacks) and

Puerto-Ricans that live in the inner-cities (Ghettos).

It is easy for me to concentrate on the ghetto, because that is where I'm from. I understand the issues that plague the ghetto, and I am a product of the social conditioning that breeds prejudice and animosity towards the adversity of those outside of the ghettos. My wife came up with the title; "A Window in Da' Hood," because that is exactly how I wrote this book. I sat in my living room, and looked outside my window, and wrote down what I saw. I will use what I saw as an explanation as to why minorities are not involved in the animal rights struggle.

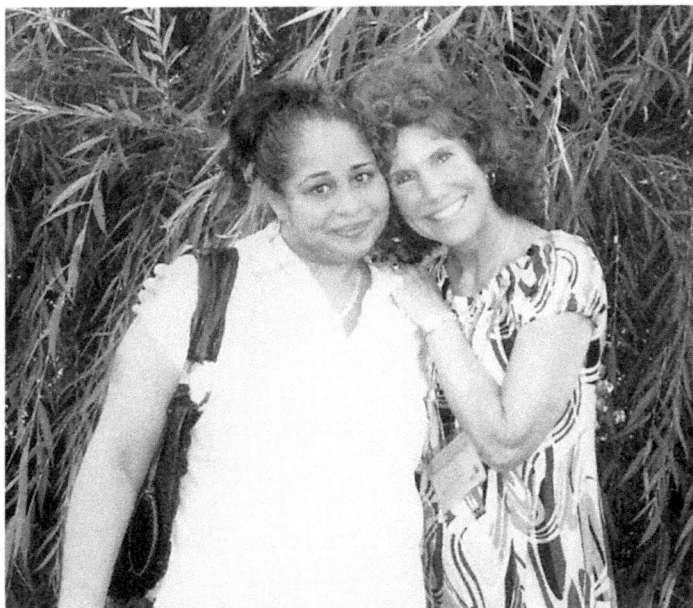

I wrote the introduction last, in order for me to give you an idea of what you can expect to read. You can expect a harsh truth about the things we face in "Da' Hood," that distracts us from seeing what goes on outside of "Da' Hood." You can expect to come to an understanding of why minorities in the inner-city shun anything that is telling them that it's wrong to eat meat, and wear animal products. And finally, you will understand our need to have animal activists to come into the inner-city to 'broaden our horizon.'

With all that said, let me thank you for reading my work. Without you, this book wouldn't exist. Enjoy reading.
--Mr. Eldon Brown

Chapter One

Creating a New Thought Pattern.

Last night, my wife and I were looking out of the window talking when we saw something that bothered us both immensely. There is a 'Pit-Bull' in our neighborhood named Macy. She is a really sweet, powerfully-built dog, which everyone in the area knows. Unfortunately for Macy, her owner is an irresponsible ghetto foster mother that will allow anyone to walk her.

Well, about 6:00pm last night there were approximately nine children in front of an associate's house in the middle of the block. These children, aged from 12-17, had a water hose taking turns antagonizing the dog by spraying her with the water hose. The dog was getting angrier by the moment, and began jumping at the children attempting to bite them. And the saddest part about the whole episode is, a couple of the children's parents were sitting there laughing at this horror show. Now, the dog is extremely enraged by now. She's jumping at the child that is spraying her with the hose, and the other children are picking up sticks and bottles to hit her with. So, my wife gets the phone and calls the homeowner to let him know what's taking place in front of his house. She hangs up the phone, and we watch as he immediately puts an end to the nonsense. But, we were sad to realize that the home owner was sitting right there on the porch watching the whole thing laughing as well.

What these parents can't seem to understand, is that silence is condoning. When children are acting out is such disruptive manners, and the parents are just sitting there watching, and laughing they are not simply condoning, they are also encouraging these actions. What this tells me is that we must work on educational programs for these parents while working with the children.

Unfortunately, these parents are following a tradition of 'moral bankruptcy.' I am talking about parents that teach their children to "get yours," when speaking about topics such as 'public assistance' (because here, getting a job is not usually a topic).

We know this couple named 'Cookie & Jose,' who take turns applying for emergency foods-stamps each month, averaging a little over $500 a month. That's six thousand taxpayer dollars a year, being manipulated from the city of New York. And that's just one couple. We know numerous people that do this every month, and it's a multi-million dollar a year scam being perpetrated against the state, by the people getting the food-stamps and the stores that change them for cash at 50% its value. These scams are taught to inner-city children at a very young age as a means of survival, instead of teaching them self-determination.

Because this is the norm within the inner-city, the job of teaching these parents that their actions are counter-productive to their children is extremely tedious. But, it can be done. It would have to be done by teaching the value of true self-determination.

That job becomes even more tedious with the Democratic Party constantly expanding, and increasing food-stamps and other welfare "benefits." The state's willingness to give these free 'give aways,' is increasing this belief in entitlement.

I remember reading a study done on president Lyndon B Johnson's so-called "war on poverty," with its "great society program." The study showed that, with all the government sponsored community programs, there still was a 4 million increase in public assistance applications.

This increase shows that over 4 million people developed a "why work when the government will give us money?" attitude. Another example of what I'm speaking about is a girl we know named Leslie.

Leslie is having children like its some type of fashion statement. All of her children have different fathers, and she chooses not to deal with any of them. She receives

12

public assistance for all of her children. She walks around wearing $500 Versace glasses, while her children walk around looking like a bunch of derelicts. Section 8 pays her rent, and she sells her children's social security numbers every year for $500 apiece during tax time (the way this works is, she gets $500 for letting someone claim a child on their taxes as a dependant).

These types of ghetto dwellers are parasitic individuals that were taught how to "beat the system." However, although the parents are the major cause of these disgusting practices, the states greatly contributes to these inner-city norms by creating a welfare system designed to make people lazy and dependant upon the state. And any community organization that is geared towards working with inner-city minorities has to face this problem.

Inner-city minorities don't seem to realize the positive role models that are out there, when these parents fall short, (as they often do), of their responsibilities. For the young girls out there, we have women like Whoopi Goldberg, and Oprah Winfrey plastered all over the airwaves. From my understanding, these two women didn't grow up with silver spoons in their mouths. I believe that they both have overcome extraordinary obstacles to reach their astounding levels of success, thus making them both perfect role models for young women to emulate.

However, these inner-city parents don't teach their daughters to view these women as true success stories, and use them as a source of inspiration for their offspring's. They would rather teach them to chase drug

13

dealers, and manipulate the system.

Let me share another story with you, which relates to this topic of misguided adults, and the manner in which they misguide the youth.

My wife and I were sitting outside with our neighbor, and her 9yr old granddaughter. Another tenant came downstairs (an older woman around 50yrs old), and told the child:
"..You know that old drunk that lives upstairs? Well, when he comes home, I'm going take his money and give you some. That's how you got to do it!"

I looked at her as if her had had fallen off! But, before I could respond my wife had countered her ignorance by telling the little girl:
"..No, you come from great people. People that have struggled so that you can have all the things that you enjoy today. I want you to love school, so that you will have the education that you need to accomplish your goals when you get older. I want you to promise me that you will always treat people the way that you want them to treat you, with respect and kindness."

The reason Katie countered the idiotic rants of this parasite, was to give this child a positive perception on how to deal with people, thus challenging the negativity that this insignificant feminine organism, was attempting to put in this child's young mind. And this is another obstacle that we have to face when trying to educate our youth, the indoctrination of social misfits.

And let me make something absolutely clear. When
14

I say "social misfits," I am not speaking of "deviant behavior." I am speaking of those whom have been ostracized by their peers due to their irrational and ignorant character. That being said let me continue.

We must continuously counter the ignorance of the parents, to change the thought patterns of our youth. And we must keep in mind that the immoral characteristics displayed by these parents didn't just start today. It's just that so many things that we accept today, was shunned 30 or more years ago. I will use a personal story as an example of what I am speaking about.

I grew up in an extremely dysfunctional family. My mother was a crack addict, and a prostitute. And my step-father (who is also my mothers first cousin), was very physically abusive. One day, when I was eleven years old my step-father asked me to go to the store to get him a pack of cigarettes. After I bought the cigarettes, I took the change, which was a quarter and played a game of "Donkey Kong."

When I gave my step-father his cigarettes, he asked me for his change. I got scared by the way he had asked for his change, so I lied and said that I was hungry so I bought a twinkie. He knew that I was lying, and told me that he knew that I was in the pizza shop playing Donkey Kong. He then told me to go into the bedroom and take my clothes off, because he was going to "bust my ass for lying." I did as I was told, but I was hoping that my mother was going to intervene because she heard the whole incident.

Well she didn't. My step-father came into the room, tied

me up, and he beat me, and beat me. He beat me long and hard. He beat me until blood was running down my back. He beat me until I couldn't cry anymore. He beat me until I urinated and defecated on myself. And he didn't stop beating me until my mother finally walked into the bedroom, and asked; "are you going to kill him?"

When he stopped I got up, walked into the bathroom, ran a hot tub of water and sat there in excruciating pain. I sat there emotionally numb, and promised myself that no one will ever beat me again without paying severe and deadly consequences (and if you know me, you will be assured that no one has ever beat me since).

However, this brutal attack against me is very common in the inner-cities of America. The drug addiction, unemployment, and moral bankruptcy add up to abuse. Now you try to contemplate my response to animal abuse after taking an ass whipping like I just described to you.

The saddest part of this story is that there are thousands of children faced with these obstacles. These children, who are in desperate need of nurturing, seek that nurturing in the streets. If there were people out there that they see doing positive things, it will show them a life beyond despair and help them aspire to be a part of positive change.

As adults, with the exception of those who eventually become self educated, the rest is only capable of teaching what they have learned themselves, and you see what they have learned. Unfortunately most of these parents (who are children themselves), comes from a sub-culture

That's lacking in education, a religious foundation, or anything resembling the concept of' 'community.'

We grow up believing that gangs are family, women are bitches, and friends are niggers. We are taught that law enforcement is our enemies. If a child in the ghetto tells his/her mother that they want to be a cop when they grow up, the parents response is likely to be: "stop talking stupid!"

I remember when I was a child; I had told my eldest brother that I wanted to be a 'fire-man' when I grew up, and he told me to, "Stop talking like a fucking pussy!" The fact remains that we must reach the adults in our inner-city communities, and teach them about how the negative affects of their lack of education and morality is truly hurting the our future generations. And we need to show those who claim to be educated, that they are also in need of direction.

An example of the need for the so-called educated minorities to find direction was the presidential election. Great numbers of minorities came out to vote for Barak Hussein Obama, simply because he's black.

To vote for a president because he is black; and not based on his ideals and track record as a senator, is not only a form of reverse racism; it is also an act of pure stupidity. Instead of contributing to reverse racism, we should be focused on teaching these ignorant adults some self-determination, so they can stop selling their children's social-security numbers and being social parasites.

We need to focus on teaching these mis-educated illiterate parents to stop telling their daughters that they should use the "shelter system to get section 8 quicker."

We need to teach these parents that allowing their young daughters to dress extremely provocative, is also allowing them to be disrespected. Because how an individual dresses is also a reflection of their personality. We need to show these parents that allowing their sons to go outside with their pants hanging below their buttocks, is also allowing them to degrade themselves.

Most importantly, we must find a way to teach these parents that they can be somebody themselves if they just take the time to look in the mirror. They must find their own sense of self-worth. We must show these parents that if they are willing to chase their dreams, that their dreams can become a reality. We can show them that they can contribute to their community, and make a difference in their lives, as well as the lives of their children.

And when we accomplish this daunting task, we will witness a change in their thought patterns. These parents will become analytical, and therefore begin to make conscious decisions. They will begin to look at the "pros & cons" of their actions, as well as the actions of their children. They will begin to question what they eat, and how what they eat affects them 'mind & body.' With a clear mind and goal orientated, we can then approach these parents about the diverse struggles that are going on around them, which they are blind to. And one of the struggles that we can then enlighten them to is the struggle for Animal Rights and Animal Liberation.

We can begin with little things, like what is fact or fiction about drinking milk, or why is it that black people have a much higher rate of high blood pressure, and diabetes than any other ethnic group in

America. Then maybe, we'll slow down (or stop) eating so much fried-chicken, and other animal foods & animal by-products that's counter-productive to our health.

And let me assure all animal activists out there, the animal rights movement has never seen the likes of activism like minorities are capable of bringing to the table. We are passionate, devoted, and extremely aggressive. We simply need to find a way to direct all that pent up energy and the misery that exist within our sub-culture, and direct it at a target; and that target will get hit.

The inner-city (ghetto) is no place for children to be raised. The heartache and despair, the drug addictions, and child negligence, the lawlessness, and the lack of education; is all due to poverty, immorality and a lack of self-determination. The mis-education is due to false leadership, by individuals capitalizing off of the heartache and despair that comes with poverty. We have leaders like Alfred Charles Sharpton (Al Sharpton), who rose to power due to a lying whore who didn't want to get her ass whipped by her parents, so she lied and told everyone she was bound and raped by six white men, whom were police officers. They caused a national uproar, caused a man to lose his life, and almost caused a racial riot throughout America.

He knew this bitch was lying, but spearheaded the "Tawana Brawley Movement" anyway. Sharpton was recorded telling Brawley's attorneys Alton Maddox, and C. Vernon Mason;" if we win this case we will be the biggest niggers in America!" and yet, in October 1988 when everyone found out that this idiot girl was lying, instead of locking these clowns up, he was glorified as some type of negro hero.

To make matters worst, this same so-called "leader" attempted to put Nicole Pultrie Bell in a councilwoman's seat in Queens new York, in 2010. Let's reflect back for a second on who Bell is. On November 25, 2006, Sean Bell (Nicole Pultrie Bells' Fiancé and "babies daddy"), was at a bachelor party with two friends fighting over who was going to take a stripper home. Sean Bell said he was going to his car to get his "gat" (gun). This comment was over heard by an undercover NYPD officer, and when Bell and his friends got in the car, the officer identified himself, and told them to stop. Instead of complying, Sean Bell tried to run the officer over, which resulted in Bell being killed and his two friends being injured.

The incident resulted in Nicole Pultrie Bell getting over 3 million dollars in settlement money, and over 250 thousand dollars in federal grant money for a non-profit organization. The other two wannabe gangsters also received large settlements. This was all due to Al Sharptons' ability to make a mockery of the system. And according to him, this incident also qualifies this 'hood-rat' to run for public office.

Here are the biggest problems with these "nigger

leaders," their only around when they can agitate the public for self exposure. Their never around when minorities really need them. A prime example of this is told in the September 7th issue of the New York daily news. There is an article there covering the story of a five year old kindergarten student that went to the school bathroom, and was held down by two other children (1rst. graders), and molested by a third child.

Where in the hell were the Rev. Al Sharpton and the other "community leaders" for these families? Where was the organizing of psychological support for the tormented five year child? Where was the agitation of the community to formulate programs designed to combat these extreme forms of morbid mayhem!? They didn't see how the incident benefited them, so they ignored it. It was more important to put an expensive suit on somebody's "babies momma," have her run for a menial political position (so they can solicit state funds), then to help a helpless, traumatized five year old. Now, do you still wonder why; "how come there aren't many minorities in the animal rights struggle?"

For the entire animal activist population that has asked the above question, let me say; I've once read that "the best way to take care of yourself is to take care of those who can take care of you." And I whole heartedly agree with that comment. When we assist those in need, we are showing them that helping others creates a better society. And most people will show their gratitude by helping those who have extended their hands to them.

The number of animal rights activist out there ranges in the hundreds of thousands. If they were to put minimal resources into assisting inner-city community organizations, that's geared towards teaching our youth self-determination and community development, they will be pleasantly surprised by how the change in thought patterns will bring them many new recruits in the animal rights struggle.

Chapter Two

Why Animal Rights are Needed.

Let's do a little study of our own. We'll start with a quick study of something most people seems to enjoy eating, which is 'Shrimps.'

Ecological Fact: the leg movements of shrimps serve the purpose of collecting algae, bacteria, protozoa, rotifers, and floating detritus from the water. They filter food from the water by scraping their appendages against waste matter, and then eat the waste. Shrimps also eat dead tadpoles, mollusks, as well as amphibian eggs. Point being? They literally clean the oceans for us, and they never overpopulate due to large whale consumption.

The catching of millions of pounds of shrimps yearly

for human consumption is causing immense pollution in our waters. Will having this tidbit of knowledge about shrimps, make you think twice about purchasing this so-called delicacy?

I don't have enouh ink, paper, or knowledge to document the many diverse roles that the animal kingdom plays in contributing to the growth of our environment. So instead, I will very briefly state a couple of facts about the health risk of meat and dairy products. I will begin with Milk.

Contrary to what the Food and Drug Administration (FDA), wants us to believe about how healthy milk is supposed to be for us, studies have shown that drinking milk actually causes acid to ride in your blood level, and our natural defense to this rise in acidity, is taking calcium from our bones to neutralize the extra acid.

According to Dr. Neal Bernard (president of the committee for responsible medicine), osteoporosis is caused by five factors that forces calcium from the bones, and that is:
"..animal protein, caffeine, sodium, tobacco, and sedentary life-styles."

It has been proven that avid milk drinkers have a much higher risk at getting osteoporosis then non-milk drinkers, and vegans even less. Not only does consuming animal protein destroy our bones, it increases our chances for heart attacks, strokes, and slows down our digestive tracks and also clogs major arteries.

Eating meat increases the risk for women to develop

25

breast cancer, as well as increase's chances for men to get prostate cancer at much younger ages. And let us not forget that most of the pesticides that are consumed by people come from eating meat. Also, it has been proven that the breast milk from mothers that eat meat contains levels of pesticides that are harmful to their children.

Most people in America are so focused on providing their families with basic primal needs (food, clothing, and shelter), that they embrace anything that the government tells them is good for them. Proof of this is how people embrace the FDA's "Food Pyramid" nonsense, with its four food groups. The FDA developed what they called the "food guide pyramid," to replace the "four food groups" of the 1950's, as a way to give more variety in what they want us to believe is a balanced diet.

The first part consists of; bread, cereal, rice, and pasta. The second part consists of; fruits, and vegetables. The third part consists of; milk, yogurt, and cheese. And the fourth part consists of; meat, and fish. I have to say that they were doing quite well until they got to the third part, with all of its trans-fat to clog your arteries, and its high cholesterol to give you high blood pressure, with a little taste of heart disease for desert!

I definitely see the need for minorities to stop, look, and listen to animal rights activist. And if you're not willing to listen for the sake of your health, due to years of being brainwashed, then I'll attempt to appeal to your conscious.

Like us, animals are sentient beings. They love, and they know when they are loved. They feel fear, and know when they are threatened. They feel sorrow, as well as joy. They feel hunger, and know when they are full. They fight to protect their young (shit, some of us don't even do that!). They seek shelter from storms, and even groom their young.

What they don't have is a voice. A voice to say; 'stop, you're hurting me.' A voice to beg; 'please don't kill my child!' a voice to say; 'there's another to test your drugs.' And a voice to ask; 'why are you killing us, when we've done nothing to you?'

Just as God is the voice of the voiceless for those who embrace religious doctrines, so is animal activist, the voice of the millions of voiceless animals. Just as Moses, Jesus, and Muhammad, is heart of a heartless world for those who find peace within religious dogmas, so are animal activist the speaking, protesting, and agitating hearts of the animal kingdom.

Every time that you a piece of chicken, you're devouring an animal that was once nurtured as you were once nurtured. Providing water to quench thirst, shelter to protect not only from a storm, but also from predation. We provide our children food for nourishment, just as farmers provides their animals food for nourishment. The difference is that we don't break their necks, drain their blood, cut them into pieces, and sell them for 69cents a pound. Sounds barbaric don't it? Well, it gets worst, but I believe you get my point.

We are compassionate by nature (or atleast we are supposed to be). So, you would think that compassion for animals would be inherently in us. Unfortunately, social indoctrination has stripped us of our "humanness." Now, back to minorities and their dis-interest in the animal rights struggle.

For inner-city children, animal abuse can (and many times does) become an outlet to release pent up tension. Let me explain. Growing up in the south Bronx, I have witnessed countless forms of animal abuse as a child. Let's understand that children that are raised in Americas inner-cities posses extreme inner rage. They are enraged by watching their mothers struggling alone because their fathers are nothing more than insignificant sperm donors.

They are enraged because they witness their parents fruitless attempts to escape adversity through "crack," "heroin," and "cocaine" addiction. They are enraged because every time they go to the store, they police stops and search them like their criminals. They are enraged because every time they go to school, their treated like terrorist, by being subjected to metal detectors and pat-downs. And like any other emotion, rage needs an outlet.

Unfortunately, this outlet ends up being the dogs, cats, squirrels, and pigeons that co-inhabits these communities. May it be the ignorance of a teenager throwing a pit-bull of the roof, or minors shooting

pigeons with pellet guns, these actions are all signs of these children's need to rid themselves of their inner rage. I'm not this as an excuse; I'm saying this simply to bring about an understanding. Let me use myself as an example.

I am the youngest of five children. I was raised in a very dysfunctional environment (as I expressed earlier). My mother being a crack addict, allowed my step-father to constantly molest my sisters because he was supplying her drug habit. My uncles were very violent muslims, that to this day I have no respect for, because they did nothing to protect my sisters.

At that time in my life, I had a fierce hatred toward drug dealers, due to me watching my mother constantly performing sexual favors at a very young age. And with the exception of me and my eldest sister, my mother smoked crack with all my other siblings. The pain, and anger that dwelled within the deepest spheres of my soul, was too much for me to bear. I would get migraine headaches so bad, that I would sit down, hold my head and cry until it went away. There were times when I thought my head would explode. And sadly, I would take this anger out on innocent stray animals. I'm not going to go into specifics; I'm sure that you get my point.

Again, I'm not using my anger and depression to justify inexcusable acts. I want you to understand that there are roots to these problems. And the same problems that I faced as a child, children today are facing even worst. And their releasing their inner, rage by killing each other.

Many years later sitting in a prison cell, I would question myself time, and time again on how come I became so desensitized towards everything and everyone that was outside of my immediate circle.

In my journey to understanding my willingness to embrace violence, I had to realize that violence didn't bother me due to my lifelong exposure to it. All I've ever been exposed to was violence. At home, violence was the main language used to get your pint across. Outside in the projects, violence was the number one means of making money, and even in school, the toughest kids had the most respect.

And as for my youthful insensitivity towards animals, that was due to me being exposed to dog fighting at such a young age. By my young mind witnessing such bloody brutality, it not only desensitized me to animals, but humans as well. It made me view animals as nothing more than objects for our entertainment. It made me see people as being than deceptive, and untrustworthy, and expendable. Unfortunately for both people, and animals this is a common thought amongst most people in Da' hood.

However, the main reason that people in the inner-city don't teach our children to appreciate the beauty of animals is because wearing expensive furs, and leather is a status symbol in the ghetto. Understand this, when you grow up poor, you develop your idea of what success is through media outlets.

If these outlets are constantly showing us that "successful people" are wearing 'timberlands,' 'north-face,' and 'mink coats,' then when people in Da' Hood have money they are going to by these items to show that they have money.

And it's not just with clothing, it's also with food and

where we go to eat. If people with money go to eat at particular places, then people from the inner-city wants to go to those places as well.

I remember one of the first places that I took my wife out to eat. It was this well know, and expensive restaurant called; 'Ruth's cris steak house,' trying to impress her. First of all, my Queen wasn't impressed, and secondly the food was nasty as hell! I ordered "Fillet Minon," which I knew absolutely nothing about. I grew up eating fried chicken and white rice 300 days out of the year. Nevertheless, I thought I impressed her by taking her to a place that "white people ate."

Not only was she not impressed, but the waiter had to go to the deli for some A1 steak sauce! So much for eating where "white people" ate. And now, many years later as my Queen and I have become animal conscious (or rather conscious of the animal rights struggle), I think of how many cows were murdered for Michael Jordon & Nike to team up and come out with sneakers that sells for $200 dollars a pair (and $2 to make). Then I think of all the minority children that have gotten murdered from wearing these dead cows on their feet. It's sickening, but very real.

I believe that understanding and sympathizing with animal rights activist, can play a major role in ending these types of destructive behavioral patterns by inner-city youth. It would devalue these items that their willing to die, or kill for.

Chapter Three

What is the "Black Struggle?"

What is the "Black Struggle?" let me print here an essay that my wife had written in 2010. This essay will clearly answer that question.

"We the forgotten people.

America is in an economic crisis. Well, that crisis is well understood in Da'Hood. You see, we've always wondered how we're going to pay next months rent. Others are now learning what this is like. We've always known what it's like to wonder, what we are going to eat for dinner tomorrow. Others are now learning what this is like. Budget cuts; is that what the masses in America are worried about? Well let me explain what "budget cuts" are to us in Da'Hood. When you have to buy "oodles-of-noodles," that cost five for a dollar, with a pack of associate franks, and make sure that it stretches for three meals, that's a budget cut. When Tropicana orange juice is a luxury that you can only afford once a month, so you have to settle for that sugar based "sunny delight" that's a budget cut.

When peanut butter and jelly sandwiches is the most filling meal of the day, that's a budhet cut. And when you have to eat chicken and rice 360 days out of the year, that's a budget cut. So, what the mass majority of American citizens consider to be budget cut, we've always endured.

I grew up in the red hook projects in Brooklyn, and my husband grew up in the James Monroe projects in the Bronx, and as we journey back into these lands of despair, we can't help but feel the pain of societies neglect, along with the self afflicting genocide that stems from the fact that the true leaders of these neighborhoods (or better yet, these sub-cultural dwellings of danger), are the blood, crips, Latin kings, or neitas. Everyone in these dwellings of darkness acknowledges that the preposterous politician and community activist that claim to be 'leaders,' only remember the people when it's financially beneficial for them to do so. This is the main reason why ghetto dwellers (which we are included), view everyone outside of our community as predator or prey.

And I also realize that we in 'Da' Hood' play a major role in reinforcing most of the stereo-types that causes us to be "forgotten people." Pissing in elevators, throwing garbage out of windows, leaving trash and dog shit

33

all over the streets. Our children wearing their pants down to the top of their thighs. Women sitting in public assistance offices asking for welfare, with $10,000 in jewelry on (you need to sell that and feed your damn kids!) and a blatant disrespect for anyone outside our communities.

This is what happens when babies are having babies. They can't teach them shit, because they don't know shit, and sadly they aren't trying to learn shit. But, that doesn't mean we shouldn't give a shit! I tell my people everyday to wake the hell up. I tell them that we're a forgotten people because we don't give greater society anything to remember (other than we're good at boxing, and basketball). I tell my people everyday to respect their elders, and teach their children to value education; so that they will have 'options' about how they want to live their lives when they become of age to be on their own. I tell my people everyday to believe in themselves, so that they can develop self-determination, and rid themselves of this sense of entitlement. There's not a day that goes by, that I don't tell young men to pick their pants up and walk with some morals, and self-respect. I tell them to value where they lay their heads, and stop throwing trash out of the windows, pick up after their dogs, and stop pissing in the elevators.

And a little message to the New York legislators; I want to let y'all know that we reward our children when they do good. We reward them as means of inspiration for them to continue to do good. The flip side to that is we punish them when they do bad. When there is no fear of consequences, there's more deviant behavior. What has happened (at least in New York City), is that the state government has stripped parents of their parental rights. Parents in New York City can't even discipline their children. The New York City public schools (amongst other city agencies), are giving children telephone numbers to call if they "feel their parents are abusing them." This is a very disturbing situation for parents. And parents are afraid to discipline their children.

In the minds of today's youth, "abuse" is everything from, not being able to stay out late to; "you're not going out on a school night!" And because parents today are forced to be concerned about what is politically correct child rearing, children are given too much freedom. When more conservative child rearing is used, the parents are chastised by the system and labeled as abusive. This situation has gotten so bad in New York City, that children are now threatening their parents with; "if you touch me, I'll call ACS" (Administration for child services). Or the threat that I often hear that drives me crazy; "put your hands on me, and see if I don't have you arrested." And sadly, the parents would back down in fear. This state has given our children permission to challenge us.

This is absolutely unacceptable. It is not the governments position (state, federal, or local), to raise our children, or tell us how to raise our children. And trust me, there's a great difference from 'whipping' a child, and 'abusing' a child. It is the parents' responsibility to raise, reward, and discipline their children in a manner that they see fit, in order to make their children productive members of society. How can a parent contribute to their Childs growth & development, if they fear retribution from the state, if the state disagrees with their parenting? We

35

really need to rake a stand, and tell our legislators that we don't need them dictating how we should raise our children, and stop stripping us of these fundamental rights."
Katie Liz Brown

How I love my Queen!
The reason the above essay is so profound, is that the 'Black Struggle' in America is two fold. The first struggle is against 'self,' and the second struggle is against the 'system.

Lets begin with the struggle against 'self.' Our women have lost all respect for themselves, and our men have lost all sense of responsibility. We no longer teach our children to respect our elders, nor themselves. Yet, we do teach them how to abuse the welfare system. I can not count how many women that I know, who are with their children's father and lie to their case worker about how their "baby daddies" deserted them, so that they can get cash and food-stamps. I can not count how many men that I know that have four or five "baby mommas," and don't provide for any of them. I can not count how many parents that I know, that hangs out all night whiles their under age children run the street.

As for the system, prejudice is very prevalent in our inner-cities (even with our socialist, religiously confused, black president). Minority communities are still put on the 'back-burner' when it comes to state and federal funding. Our schools still receive second hand materials. Our sanitation department doesn't take cleaning our community very seriously. Our police departments are very abusive, and still possess an "us against them" mentality. It seems as the only city agency that takes us seriously, is the fire department.

The multitude of issues faced by the minority community is too much to document here. But, the issues are wide spread and very real. So, when I'm asked; "how come we don't see that many minorities in the struggled for animal rights, and animal liberation," I would usually say that we don't have the 'privilege' to get involved.

However, if animal activist would take a moment to come into our world, and stand side by side with us in our fight against social injustice, they will find powerful allies. You will be pleasantly surprised how receptive we are to issues that are foreign to us. Animal activist should not be afraid to enter the inner-city. And if you are, contact the KLB Association and we will take you to the inner-city, and walk with you.

Chapter Four

Why Minorities Should Embrace The Animal Rights Struggle.

We all know that language in one of the most important factors in the process of social change. The ability to communicate creates the understanding needed for others to understand our trails and tribulations, and vice versa and together produce a common solution for our problems. Without language there would be no friendship, there would be no concept of marriage; and there would be no such thing as community.

We use language everyday in our daily activities may it be work or play, some of us even take the time to learn other languages in order to communicate with those who speak other languages as a way to expand their horizons. Language is used to inform us of the past. For example, if you want to know what people contributed to the destruction of African civilization, all you have to do is study linguistics. Every language on the face of the earth is unique to a particular people. If we look at the dominant language throughout most of Africa we will see that it's Arabic. Now Arabic is a Semitic language with no African origins, and yet it is the main language in Egypt, Algeria, Sudan, the entire central Africa, and northern Africa. What this tells us, is that it was the Arab world not, the Europeans that destroyed and colonized that continent. After the Muslim prophet had Muhammad died, the caliphate under Umar the great had invaded Africa, and declared jihad (holy war), on all who did not embrace monotheism. This beginning of Arabic in African language, is the proof of that fact that language is without a doubt, one of the most important characteristics that humans possess. Language allows one generation to transliterate their story to the next generation, creating what we know as legacy. We express our language in the most complex ways of all sentient beings … our voice. But what will happen if we didn't have our voices?

This is a question well under stood amongst Africans Americans. we have suffered more oppression, rapes, murders, and lynchings than all other people on the face of this earth combined. For hundreds of years our voices have been ignored by both God, and man alike. It wasn't until we added violence to our voice that we began to be heard, and supported by others whose voices were heard.

The power of language is what gives individuality. If something has language, that something becomes someone. Because you can only have language with intelligence, no matter how limited that intelligence may be. And if someone posses language and intelligence, than that same someone deserve rights. With that being said, I pose the question; do animals have language? According to Daniel Ryan, of Robert Mann conservation:

"The big black crow, have noisy food calls ,assembly calls, courtship calls, and a lot of squabbling over roosting spots, as they settle down for the night....."

The above mention quote is purely a sign of language, and intelligence. When my wife tells me that dinner is ready, she is giving me a food call. When animal rights activists have a conference, they are giving an assembly call, and as my wife and I are joking around while getting ready for bed, we are squabbling as we settle down.

I can give countless examples of animal intelligence, especially where primates are concern. but my point of writing this book is to find the means of getting minorities interested in the struggle for animal rights and animal liberation, and vice versa. In order for me to accomplish this goal, I must first show why minorities feel that our struggle is different from the struggle for animal rights, and animal liberation, I think I've done a fair job of that already, and I must expound on the discrimination that I've personally found to exist within certain groups in the animal rights movement.

Three years ago my wife introduces me to the animal liberation struggle. She was going Christmas shopping the day after thanksgiving to catch all the sales, and past by an animal rights protest by a group known as "W.A.R" (win animal rights). After speaking to some of the protestors, and seeing what the group stood for, she became excited about this organization. As with everything else that we do, we discussed the topic at length, and I told her I'll do some research about it.

While doing my research, I was truly amazed at what I was reading. This was a whole new world opening up for me. Years ago, I remembered watching the news and seeing people throwing paint on people wearing fur coats. But, I just thought: 'look at those crazy people; they don't have nothing better to do!' I never took it seriously. I would watch it, and burst out laughing. Now, I'm at the computer reading about all these people taking risk, and making sacrifices for the rights of animals. I was truly impressed. And I also realized that the animal rights movement just recruited an extremely rugged individual, me…that is, if my wife lets me.

My Queen, as tough as she is, loves her some animals. And remember when she would share her childhood stories about growing up in Puerto-Rico, and her father would take her to "cock-fights." She would tell me how she would cry every time a rooster would die. Her heart was too pure to become desensitized.

Anyway, she was extremely happy to hear that I would do more than just support her in this endeavor. She knew that I would become active in getting the message out, about the animal liberation struggle. Being that she signed the registration form with W.A.R., they sent us emails on all their activities, inviting us to join. So, we decide to join a protest that next weekend at the home of some guy named 'Andrew Baker.'

The Saturday of the protest, my wife was feeling ill. She told me that she would be alright and that she really wanted me to go to the protest so that I can see what its like. She told me to ask for a woman named 'Camille Hankins,' because she had spoken to her on the day she first stopped at their protest, and told Camille about me.

I made it to the gathering place, at 59th street and Columbus circle about 15-minutes early. I took a seat facing central park, and just enjoyed the scenery until I saw people begin entering thee circle. I saw two women walk in the circle holding signs in their hands, and both had on t-shirts with a dog holding guns. Obviously to me, they were W.A.R. protesters. And this is where the nonsense begins.

I walk over to the two women and introduce myself, and ask: 'are y'all here for the W.A.R. protest?' They looked at each other, then said no and walked away. I went back to my spot, sat back down and continued waiting. I noticed the two women kept staring back at me. Now, I knew these two women were with the group I was waiting for. But, I took into consideration that this is New York, and I'm a very big Blackman, and very big black men don't just walk up to two little white women, and start asking questions.

Now, I must admit that I'm not exactly "tall, dark, and handsome." At 6'1 320lbs, with ear rings in both ears, tattoos on both sides of my face, scars on both my face, and head, I could understand their initial skepticism. I mean, even police place their hand close to their firearm when I walk towards them. So, maybe the women were a little afraid.

However, about ten minutes go by and other group members begin walking in with their signs, and the two women gathered with them, and they all began talking. I knew what their group leader (Camille) looked like, from the internet so I decided to wait for her to save myself a headache.

One of the women that I had approached was talking to the group, and pointed at me. Everyone turned and looked at me, then turned back around and resumed talking. Now, I'm getting angry, so I walk over to the group and ask; "is there a fuckin' problem?" some stocky guy (who I would later know as Matt) answered: "there's no problem big man. Are you here for the protest?" I responded very nasty and said: 'I'm sure these two little girls already told you that!'

He eased some of my anger when he responded, very softly saying: 'we'll be getting started as soon as Camille gets here. It's nice to meet you, and held out his hand. I didn't shake his hand; I just turned around and walked back to where I was sitting.'

I noticed a few of them kept glancing my way, and I gave them a look that I know made the souls tremble. I really wasn't up for the nonsense. If I would have known that these people were clown, I would have stayed home and tended to my Spanish Queen, like I would usually do if she's feeling under the weather. Anyway, I sat there until Camille Hankins arrived.

When Camille Hankins finally arrived, her "followers" surrounded her and started talking. I walked over to introduce myself. I told her that she had already met my wife at 'fur-free-Friday.' To my surprise, she responded by asking: "Is she a pretty little redhead about my height?" I told her that was my baby, and she didn't come because she wasn't feeling well. But, she'll be at the next protest. Camille said she understood and hopes she gets better. She must have felt my tension, because she asked me was everything aright?

I told her no it wasn't, and explained to her what had taken place between me and her group before she came. Camille told me not to take it personal because they're skeptical about all newcomers, due to the federal investigation that they're under. I listened to what she said. But, I also know that there's absolutely no way that I can be mistaken for a law enforcement official. I let that one go, and accepted the fake "hellos," and "nice to meet yous," from this group of 'internet impressers.' And believe me; they only impress people on the internet.

Camille Hankins began giving out signs to those of us that didn't have any. We then proceeded to our destination. On the way, the W.A.R. members avoided me like I had the bubonic plague. I had to wonder if it was because I look rough, or was it because I was the only black person in the group. Eventually, I would find out that it was both.

Since that initial meeting, I've been to various protests with various animal rights organizations, and although other groups (most of them) was welcoming, the racist attitude of the all-white W.A.R. always stuck with me.

And no, I'm not one of those "Brothers" that that cry 'racism' whenever something goes wrong. Using this particular incident as an example, lays in the reality that the animal rights movement only stagnates its growth when it displays these types of prejudice. And although W.A.R. is not the 'spokesman' for the whole animal rights struggle, they are viewed by a large internet audience.

Because most of the animal rights groups consist mostly of people of privilege, they need to rid themselves of these xenophobic types of attitudes. The struggle for animal rights is a just cause. And like any other just cause, you need sympathizers of every ethnicity to succeed. And by showing discriminatory practices, it becomes counter-productive to the growth of the movement; not to mention the fact that discriminatory practices creates unknown and un-necessary enemies.

It is my opinion, that the minority struggles in America should work hand-in-hand with the animal rights struggle, and vice versa. In doing so we will both become stronger, and increase our chances of success.

Chapter Five

Eugenic Breeding

Of the thousands of pages that I have read pertaining the north American slave trade, the most troubling for me was about the hundreds of years of 'eugenic breeding' that we were subjected to.

I can recall the first time the subject of "stud farms" crossed my path. I was incarcerated at the Clinton 'Correctional Facility' in Danamora New York. I was walking in the yard talking to the leader of the 5% Nation of Islam about a dissertation by Austrian philosopher Friedrich W. Nietzsche on "Ubermensch".. better known as "the over- man."

After reading Nietzsche book; "and thus spoke zarathustra," I was on a mission to understand what it would be like if man concentrated all his energy on the development of "self." At the time when I read the book, I understood Nietzsche to be saying that if man focused on developing the discipline needed to conquer 'desire,' and self-restraint; then he will transcend the norm. The 'norm' being, greed, lust, and the natural desire to dominate (atleast this is the norm where I come from).

I had just started studying, and my education wasn't good at all. I only completed the fifth grade in public school, and educated myself during my incarceration. So, reading these books really captivated me but, also confused me due to my lack of education. So, the understanding that I got from reading Nietzsche, was that he was considered 'un-conventional.' I believed that Nietzsche was trying to tell the world that if man mastered himself he can bring out his highest potential. And that because we're so 'beastlike' in our manner of thinking, that all we do is constantly find means of creating mass destruction.

And justify our oppressive and hypocritical behavior with religion. And that once we accept the fact that "God is dead," we would have to re-think our value system, laws, and governing strategies, based upon the values of those who have mastered 'self.' This way we can work on developing moral standards, and social norms that would be productive to the masses. And those people, both men & women, are considered "ubermensch." Those are the individuals that have come to the realization that man praises his own creation "God." They have rid themselves of that form of asinine thinking, and are motivated by a love of this world and life. This is what I understood of Nietzsche's dissertation (I say 'dissertation because the book is written in the form of a bunch of essays).

So, after listening to speak at length, the 5%-er told me that if I wanted to understand Nietzsche I would have to study "eugenic breeding." When I asked him what that was, he just told me to research it. I did. I was really amazed at my new-found knowledge, and read every piece of literature that I could find on the topic. Now, I'm not going to try and turn this into some type of ghetto biology course, but I will briefly try to explain eugenic breeding.

Eugenics is simply the belief that 'pure breeding' brings about the strongest attributes in a species (man or animals), both mentally and physically.

Although many associate eugenic breeding with Nazi Germany, its origins trace back to early Christianity. Although the term 'eugenic' was given by 'Francis Galton' in his book "Hereditary Genius," what make this topic so interesting (and disturbing) is that eugenics was widely used during the trans-Atlantic slave trade.

Slave masters in America had "stud farms," that was used strictly for breeding. These slave owners would purchase the biggest and darkest slaves, house them in barns and only use them to impregnate female slaves, due to their belief that they would produce bigger and stronger slaves, increasing their market value.

Many in the scientific field today believe that this is the reason why African Americans excel so greatly in physical sports, as well as our bodies ability to heal more

48

rapidly than other races. However, eugenic breeding is an abomination, and testament to man's ability to be purely evil. Just the thought of eugenics explains why we have no 'natural predator.' Our seemingly inability to reason will bring about our extinction.

The creation of "stud farms" is an act of continuous rape. Humans are creatures that act upon their attraction to others. To constantly force the rape of multitudes of women for financial gain, is morbidly despotic, and shows the barbarism that black women were subjected to under European imperialism.

The practice of eugenic breeding should be abolished. Like humans, animals have mating times. They have a process of attracting the opposite sex. These methods differ amongst animals, but they all have them. There is absolutely no need for eugenic breeding.

The practice of eugenic breeding is done everyday by pig farmers. Pigs have been shown to have greater intelligence than dogs (and trust me dogs are very intelligent). And the conditions of these "stud farms" are disgusting. According to Tom Reagan:
"Breeder sows, weighing as much as 400lbs, are confined to two foot wide stalls for most of their breeding lives; Which can be as long as four years."

These unnatural living conditions are extremely stressful on these innocent victims of mass savagery. To use another quote from Tom Reagan's book, 'Empty Cages':
"..sores, tumors, ulcers, puss pockets, lesions, cysts, torn ears, swollen legs everywhere, roaring, groaning,

49

tail biting, fighting and other vices as they are called in the industry. Frenzied chewing on bars, and chains or nothing at all. Stereo-typical rootinh and nest building with imaginary straw, and social defeat, lots of it, every third or fourth stall. Some completely broken being you know is alive only because he blinks and stares up at you. Creatures beyond the power of pity to help or indifference to making more miserable. Dead to the world, except as heaps of flesh."

The barbaric treatment of these animals, are inexcusable. One can only try to rationalize these actions by saying that the farmers are only doing what they were taught; and that they are de-sensitized because they were always taught that these actions are normal. To them, these actions are just as normal as they were for the slave masters.

I don't accept these actions as normal for the slave masters, and I don't accept them as normal for pig farmers. Normal is not justification for wrong period! I can't stress enough that animal are sentient beings, with feelings and intelligence.

Because they don't have a voice doesn't mean they shouldn't have rights. Animal rights groups need to band together to attack this issue. Animals have matting rituals that they use which allow for their continuous procreation. There is absolutely no need for eugenic breeding.

Chapter Six

Something All Animal Activists Need to Remember

Y'all were not always animal activists. Y'all were not always vegans, and y'all were not always conscious of animal exploitation. Y'all were not always at war with these massive conglomerations, which financially back these animal projects that's responsible for the deaths of hundreds of millions of animals every year.

Remembering this fact, might just help y'all when speaking to people that eat meat, and wear animal products. I have been to demonstrations where people would walk by, and literally be assaulted for wearing furs. Animal activist really need remember that these people are not conscious of the animal abuse that is going on. Most people that purchase furs or minks are buying them under the impression that they are making a fashion statement.

In a materialistic society, such as ours, these possessions are a status symbol. They are oblivious to the cruel and inhumane treatment that these animals suffer at the hands of these savages selling their products. By attacking them, y'all are making them shy away from the struggle.

Yon can not enlighten somebody about your struggle by attacking them…especially in public. You automatically put them on the defensive end. In order to change the way these individuals view wearing furs, activist must take the time to educate them about the horrors of the fur trade. And because these horrors are so profound, wearing them is immoral. In order to get them to sympathize with y'all struggle (and you must do that), you must develop a method to attract them, and then appeal to their consciousness.

And then we might see a change in the attitudes of the people that are purchasing these slaughtered animals. It's likely that many will become activist themselves. Just because they finally realize how much they contributed to such mass slaughter.

It seems as if animal activist forgot that they once upon a time, enjoyed a 'bacon & egg' sandwich. They forgot that they once upon a time, enjoyed the warmth of a heavy leather coat. They seem to have forgotten that they once upon a time, enjoyed the support of a nice pair of leather boots. Animal activist seem to have forgotten that once upon a time, they enjoyed some nice cold milk with their breakfast cereal. And somewhere in their life's journey, someone (or something) enlightened them to the atrocities taking place within the animal industries.

When animal activist look back, and reflect on how they were first introduced to the struggle for animal rights, they would think twice about throwing paint on someone (word of advice; don't throw any paint on minorities. We really do fight back).

The bottom line is that animal activist must reflect on their own humble beginnings. By reflecting on their beginnings, they would be aware that most people are indoctrinated to believe that it's healthy to eat meat, and those wearing furs, minks, and leather are doing so as a status symbol.

I recall back in 2005, I bought my Queen a 'Dooney & Burk' purse for $450, and everywhere she went with that purse, people gave her VIP treatment. Why? Because they assumed she was very well off financially. It is very unfortunate that we live in a society that places such high value on an individuals worth, based upon the material possessions that an individual has. But, that's how it is. We can accept it, or we can try to change it. If we decide to try and change it, then we must do so in a manner that won't put people on the defense. Remember, your objective is to get people to embrace your message, not to declare you as an enemy.

Chapter Seven

"Direct Action"

Direct Action means different things to different people. Some believe in non-violent direct action, and others believe in violent direct action. What both schools of thought have in common is that both believe in going out and facing their opposition directly. And in reality, both schools of thoughts create tangible results.

Non-violent direct action is a tool that is needed to fight for legislation that would protect the rights of animals (especially where animal cruelty is concerned), and animal habitats. The animal rights movement is truly in need of obtaining experienced and tenacious lobbyists. Many animal rights activist believe that they can't challenge the billion dollar corporations (with their high powered attorneys) in courts, or that Congress would give them the 'time-of-day.' Well, as a Blackman in America, I'm very grateful to those in the civil rights struggle that didn't have such a defeatist attitude. I'll tell you, I never thought that I will live to see the day where we would have a black president.

Nevertheless, lobbying is a very potent form of direct action. It brings to our governments attention the dissatisfaction, of the cruelty, and barbarism involved in the animal industries. The people do have a voice, and the peoples voices must be heard if the government wishes to maintain any semblance of peace.

Violent direct action also serves a purpose. Especially where vivisectors are concerned. Vivisectors have absolutely no regard for the lives of animals. They believe that animals are nothing more than "property" to be exploited for capital gain. These cowards are no better than the slave owners of American history, or the savages of Nazi Germany. They care about nothing but money. Destroying the property of these vivisectors will show them that there are consequences to their actions.

Because these savage vivisectors continue to murder, and torture millions of sentient beings for material gain, these gains should be taken away from them by any means necessary. They need to understand that people are extremely opposed to their actions, and will strike back in defense of these innocent animals. Violent direct action will enforce the will of the people upon these cruel murderers. Those that oppose violent direct action are in dire need of a history lesson.

All throughout history, we witness countless accounts of

violence used to achieve freedom, justice, and equality. From the Peloponnesian wars, to the American slave revolts, violence has been successfully used to break the chains of oppression. No one can deny the attention that violent direct action brings to any group. Violence causes people to listen. Violence wakes people up to atrocities long ignored. Violence captivates people.

Just look how billions of dollars of dollars are made yearly off of violence. Movies, music, and video games bring in untold billions by selling violence (or atleast the concept of violence). May it be the Japanese kamikaze, or the savage al Qaeda terrorist organization, violence grasp' the attention of people.

Violence is used to enforce laws, it is used as bullying tactics, and it is used as entertainment. In many instances, violence also breeds unity. Look how we New Yorkers had come together after those barbarians attacked the world trade center. Residents of New York, NYPD, the department of sanitation, teachers, stock brokers, and the exceptional sacrifices of our fire department. All came together inhaling gas and dust, sweating, crying, and helping one another, to help others.

I was in the United States penitentiary in Beaumont, Texas when the twin towers were destroyed. Tears came to my eyes (and I don't cry easily). And I realized at the moment I witnessed the carnage on the television set, of people jumping out of windows that my life would never be the same. I knew t that moment, that I would become a part of something good. I knew that the subculture that I embraced was wrong, and I must dedicate the rest of my life making things right. Yes, violence wakes people up.

When the 'Coca Cola' corporation first came out with its brand of soda, they were literally putting cocaine in their soda. The government was allowing this practice to continue for many years, because at that time cocaine was widely used in America for medical purposes. It wasn't until people that were drinking coca cola started acting out violently, that the government realized that cocaine was a powerful narcotic, and was seriously detrimental to people's health and well being. Unfortunately, it was violence that enlightened people to the destructive social behavior that cocaine causes. Personally, I don't see how people can be that naive, in this day and age about the potential benefits to violent direct action.

When my wife and I were at the 2010 animal rights convention, there was a part of the conference hosted by Mr. Darius Fulmer, pertaining to direct action. During the Q&A portion, one of the gentlemen present stated: "I respect violent direct action for many reasons. But, the fact that I don't have the guts to take those types of actions myself makes me respect those that do even more. I believe that those who oppose direct actions are too cowardly to take matters in their own hands, so they justify their cowardice with fake moral rhetoric."

That was so refreshing to hear. It was remarkable to finally hear an individual admit a truth that I already knew. Most people that oppose violent direct action only do so because they are 'non-confrontational,' or simply don't have the guts. These so-called activists remind of when I was growing up in the projects, there were a lot of guys that really tried to play the tough role. They would walk the "be-bop" walk, and they would talk the "Gangster" talk. But, when it was time to go to war, they would suddenly become "politically conscious" with:

"This is what the white man wants to see, us killing each other."

That's how these so-called non-violent activists are. They want to organize, yell, and be all over the internet making a name for themselves. But, when its time to 'step-up' to the plate, they are against violence. Let me explain something here. Protesting is agitating, and agitating opens the door to violence. Do not agitate someone if you're not prepared to deal with the consequences, period. If you're going to be the voice for the voiceless, then be ready to make sacrifices. The fight for animal rights, is not just about protesting with middle class America. Yelling in the street, only to be ignored by corporate America; or antagonized by some functional illiterate passerby.

I remember another incident that took place that really enraged me. In the early spring of 2010, Win Animal Rights had sent us an email informing us of a demonstration at the Canadian consulate in New York. I didn't think it would be a large turn out because it was on a Monday. However, when I got to the protest there was a large crowd already gathered there. I found Camille Hankins, received a banner, found my spot, and began yelling along with everyone else. After awhile, I realized that nobody was going in or out of the consulate building.

I asked one of the other organizers how come there was no activity in the building. He explained to me that the consulate was closed that day. Once again disappointed, I went and asked Camille did she know that the consulate was closed. She told me that they were on recess until Thursday. I told her to never again ask me to come to demonstration where no one is listening. It serves absolutely no purpose, and makes us look like a bunch of jackasses.

It seems as some of these organizers have nothing to do, so they take advantage of pure hearted people that really love animals, to feed their insignificant egos. It's the nature of the beast; in every social movement there will be individuals that are truly sincere, and those who will know how to manipulate them for self gratification.

However, all animal activists must understand that there are going to be different ideologies on what's best for the movement. But, y'all have the same ultimate agenda. And whatever method that you embrace as being acceptable; keep in mind that all other methods serve a purpose as well.

Direct action means different things to different people. But, it means exactly what it sounds like. To be directly involved with the actions taken to liberate animals held in captivity and to stop animal abuse, as well as animal experiments performed by these savage vivisectors... and bring it directly to those responsible for the above mentioned actions. It means taking it to the legislators that have the power to stop all these atrocities. Whatever methods that work, should be the methods that are used.

Chapter Eight

What I See

The Muslims want to build a masjid and Islamic cultural center at "Ground Zero." For those of you that don't know what "Ground Zero" is, it is where Muslim fundamentalists crashed two hijacked planes into the world trade center in New York City, reducing the buildings to rubble, and murdering 3000 people in the process. New York's mayor, Michael Bloomberg supports the construction of this masjid, and so does President Barack Hussein Obama.

The liberal media is calling anyone who doesn't support the building of this masjid a racist. But worst of all, black Americans (especially those in the Amsterdam news) went wild with accusations of "islamaphobia" (a new word). First of all, "racism" is the belief that one race is inherently superior to another. Islam is not a race, it's a religion. So nobody is being racist by not wanting a masjid built at ground zero. It's about sentiment.

Two thousand, eight hundred people were murdered by Muslims in the word trade center attack. I wouldn't give a damn if every Muslim in America denounced the attack, the fact remains that it was done by Muslims. And that being the case, to allow a masjid to be built at ground zero, is a spit in the face to every American citizen. Those Muslims didn't care who was in that building, they just wanted to kill as many Americans as possible. And yet, they feel they have the right to build a masjid in the same building where the wheels of one of the planes went crashing through the roof. And to make matters worst, our 'nigga' president speaks up for them! Hey Barack, try looking at any Palestinian newspaper dated back to September 12, 2001; see all your Muslim friends cheering the success of the 911 attacks. Obviously this clown president has some type of ultimate agenda with the Muslim world.

However, minorities have a few things that we need to fight about, instead of fighting for these hypocritical Muslims to have the rights that they won't give to others. We need to focus on fighting for the rights of our children. Let's focus on fighting for our children's health. Let's fight the FDA, to get them to tell the truth about the many health risks involved with eating meat. Let's challenge the lies that corporate America feeds us through media outlets of how we need cows' milk as a prime source of calcium.

I'm sure everyone has seen the commercial of how

"milk does the body good." Let's fight 'Kentucky Fried Chicken' to advertise how just 2.6 grams of fried chicken immensely increases your child's chances of heart disease. Let them tell you how just the skin of fried chicken, causes fat from other parts of the body to move into the belly, causing an insulin resistant state, that can lead to diabetes, high blood pressure, and the so-called "metabolic syndrome" (metabolic syndrome, is a combination of medical disorders that increase the risks for developing cardiovascular disease, and diabetes).

We need to focus more on social, animal, and environmental issues, than fighting for the rights of our first oppressors! Teaching our children about social, animal, and environmental issues will broaden their horizons, and make them more sensitive towards issues outside of "Da' Hood." These teachings will make our children more analytical, and instill within them a strong moral foundation. We tend to fight for the rights of everyone else, while constantly ignoring our own forms of self destruction. We need to clear our heads, grab a cup of coffee, and look out the living room window. Let me tell you what I see when I do this...

Last night, I was looking out the window, and I saw my wife's friend's 15yr old daughter kissing and rubbing up against older man, that looked to be in his late thirties. Just when I decided to go outside to straighten him out, the girls mother walked cross the street, and said something to the man, he reached in his pocket and gave her some money, and she walked away. Uh?

One of my elder sisters had lost all of her children,

due to her drug addiction and abusiveness. Two of her children were born with crack-cocaine in their system. And her youngest child mysteriously died at the hands of her 22yr old buy friend (she's 45yrs old by the way). Her 14yr old daughter was caught by her foster parent having sex with three adult males (two have been arrested, and the other coward can't be found). Her oldest daughter was recently released from prison for stabbing her girlfriend numerous times. And the state of New York declared her to be a fit parent, and gave her twin boys back to her.

To show how fit she is to be a parent, she cashes in her $300 in food-stamps for $150 in cash to buy her drugs. She takes her $600 social security check, and buys name brand clothes for herself, then has the audacity to ask family members for money to buy her children something to eat. And guess what? She's one of the many minorities that speaks out for the rights for Muslims to build a masjid at ground zero.

So, you have this crack addict with absolutely no morals, who abuses her offspring, abuses the system, and will verbally abuse anyone who attempts to give her constructive advice, speaking out for the rights of Muslims. This cycle is passed down from my mother. My mother created a generation of children that literally had to find means of survival at a very young age. She smoked crack with three of her five children. She allowed her husband to have sex with both her daughters, and she wore a mask in public that gave her an aura of a perfect parent. We had to survive under extremely adverse circumstances. Unfortunately for most in our next generation, they are doomed if we don't find a way

65

to intervene.

All hope is not lost, though. My eldest niece, Salima Brown, married a very nice, tenacious individual that possess positive work ethics. His name is William Hooks. Together, they have the most beautiful, happy, high spirited child that my Queen and I have ever seen. Salima is a well educated (masters degree), strong minded, beautifully stubborn woman. Katie and I can not express how proud we are of her. And no, my sister didn't create our chubby-cheeked niece to come out this way. Salima...created Salima. But she is proof that all is not lost.

Even with college degrees, they are unable to find work in their chosen fields. But, they both have "productive" employment that contributes to the growth of society and are raising little Natalie to be an amazing child. We as a people are in dire need to create programs that will produce more couples like these to phenomenal young adults so that we can have a future to be proud of.

Sadly these two are not the norm of what our inner-cities produce. Our inner-cities tend to produce social parasites like one of my elder sisters who have mastered ways of manipulating the system. She knows how to get the state to pay her rent, cable bill, buy her named brand clothes, give her money for food, and support her drug habit. And the worst part of it all is she teaches her children how to do the same.

People like this don't teach their children about a "Black struggle" (or any other struggle for that matter). And this mentality didn't just start with this generation. Ask

66

my mother how far I went in school. She was high out of her mind, she has no idea.

And today, as I look out of this window and see very young children roaming the street in the wee hours of the night, I can't help but be saddened by the knowledge of where life is going to take them. A life of immense despair, and broken dreams. A life with no direction. Contemporary nomads, wondering from place to place looking for a home, and only finding loneliness.

I believe that by introducing these children to the animal rights struggle, it would truly open their minds to a world outside of the ghetto, which can be exciting and truly fulfilling. They will begin to search for answers to questions that they never realized have so much meaning. They will seek to expand their knowledge. They will now question things outside of the ghetto. They will begin to ask; "what about human rights?" and start seeking justice, and equality. Their young minds will no longer be idle.

They will no longer have time to seek out which gang is the coolest. They will have a sense of purpose, and self-worth. They will develop a hunger for wisdom, thus decreasing the high school drop out rate. They will view their peers that involved in drugs and gangs as negative, and stray away from those destructive activities. The animal rights struggle will offer inner-city children a chance to be a part of something productive. With the help of the various animal rights groups, they can create a grassroots youth organization, where the children can see tangible results, as they enter the world of politics.

It would also improve their dietary habits. Because children tend to be more sensitive towards animal, they are more likely to desire a vegan diet, once conscious of animal suffering. And due to the passion that most animal activists seem to have, I'm more than sure they are willing to pool their resources together to accomplish such a task. The value of teaching inner-city children about the animal rights movement can not be overstated.

These youths have a lot of repressed anger, and incredible energy. Once this anger and energy is directed at a target, that target will get hit full force. We will see an impressive movement begin. The youth will force the adults to listen, in a way that we won't be able to. And not to mention seeing our future begin today. We will see our next generation develop unity, and self determination. We will see them develop discipline, and watch as they contribute to the growth of our society, and ecology. It can, and eventually will, be done. I guess the only question that remains is; who will spearhead this movement?

Chapter Nine

Our Right to Challenge What's Wrong!

When struggling to change any form of legislation (or to create new legislation), in the united states of America, the first thing that we need to do, is embrace the wisdom of the declaration of independence. In the declaration of independence, Thomas Jefferson states:

"...that to secure these fundamental rihts, governments are instituted among men, deriving their just powers from the consent of the governed. That when any form of government becomes destructive of these ends, it is the right of the people to alter or abolish it, and institute new government, laying its foundation on such principles and organizing its powers in such form, as to them shall seem most likely to effect their safety and

happiness."

There are two points here that seriously need to be addressed. The first being:
"...deriving their just powers from the consent of the governed."

What this means is that the government is to make, and enforce laws in accordance to the will of the people, and not what the government thinks is best for the people. When the people struggle for "civil rights," "gay rights," and "religious rights," we are exercising our rights as those governed , to have legislation changed, or created so that we can live our lives in a manner that's guaranteed to us by the declaration of independence, to have life, liberty, and to pursue that which makes us happy.

Black Americans should stand side by side with animal rights activist. Women's movements should stand side by side with the gay rights movements and so on. If for no other reason, then to atleast give our voices a louder battle cry. As long as a social movement is productive to the growth of society, we should support one another. This way the government must acknowledge that "we the people" have a voice, and it's the governments' obligation to govern in accordance to those voices.

If we don't learn anything else from American history, let us learn that the reason that we have an America today is because America's forefathers united to rid themselves of tyranny. It took the uniting of thirteen states and fifty five signatures to alter the course of history, and change the lives of millions. Unity truly is power, and it gives a voice to the voiceless and creates an element of limitless possibility.

The uniting of the various minority organizations with the animal rights organizations, will both enlighten each other to one another's purpose, as well as allow for the much needed "racial diversity" that will give both a stronger voice. The fact of the matter is, the same multi-billion corporations that benefits from animal cruelty, are the same multi-billion dollar corporations that are capitalizing off of exploiting minorities. Why do you think fast food corporations like McDonalds are all over the ghetto? We have five McDonalds within a five mile radius in the soundview section of the Bronx. Yet, there's only one within a 6 1/2 mile radius in Fifth Avenue in Manhattan. We must find the medium that exist between the various groups and act accordingly.

And minority social movements (especially Black organizations),must embrace the fact that there has never been a black social movement in the united states of America, that has bought about a substantial change, that did not have "white" supporters, and sympathizers. Not one. We must rid ourselves of this separatist mentality, if we are going to succeed in creating a better tomorrow for our children. Our youth don't need "reverse racism." What they are in need of is nurturing, love, and education.

Secondly, we need to pay close attention to that second part quoted from the declaration of independence:
"...that when any form of government becomes destructive to these ends, it is the right of the people to alter or to abolish it, and to institute new government,

72

laying its foundation on such principles and organizing its power in such form, as to them shall seem most likely to effect their safety and happiness."

The declaration of independence grants us, as American citizens, the right to take direct action to alter or abolish the powers that be, if said powers do not lay its foundation on principles that secures the fundamental rights of life, liberty, and the pursuit of happiness. Well, we are not safe when we attempt to exercise article 1 of the bill of rights, which states:

"Congress shall make no laws respecting the establishment of religion, or prohibiting thereof; or abridging the freedom of speech, or the press; or the riht of the people to peacably assemble, and to petition the government for a redress of grievances."

And when said rights are exercised (especially freedom of speech, and the right to assemble), we are subjected to persecution and labeled as a "Domestic Terrorist," by the same governmental powers that are supposed to protect us while where exercising our rights. So no, we're not safe. And these miscarriages of justice didn't just start now. As we journey through the epochs of American history, we witness persecution at every stage of the struggle for 'civil rights,' and 'civil liberties,' 'abortion rights,' and now 'animal rights.'

From 'Brown v The Board of Education,' to 'The Women's Liberation Movement," from 'Pedro Albiso Compose,' to Martin Luther King Jr.,' and 'William Edward Burgart Dubois,' and the list goes on. We have witnessed countless attempts by the United States government those that stood up for justice. And we must not give up until all sentient beings are free.

I do believe in the power of direct action. And what direct action means tome, is bringing the battle to your opponents doorsteps. Plain and simple. We as a people living in a society of laws possess the right to challenge any law that affects us. And if corporate America is under the illusion that they are above the law, then "we the people" have the right to shatter that illusion.

And let us not be naïve to the role that we play in allowing corporations, and government agencies to enforce laws designed to suppress those that do not fit into their 'status quo.' By the various social movements in America allowing a hiatus to exist between them, they give those in power a stronger hand to suppress.

What affects one group of people in America, affects all Americans. The perfect example of this is "Proposition 8." Proposition 8 affects all Americans, rather homosexual or heterosexual. Let me explain how.

According to the 'new Webster handy college dictionary,' marriage is defined as:
"…the state of being married or united."

Now, we can play semantics and debate its definition, or we can just acknowledge that definitions change as a society develop and becomes more multi-cultural. However, we can define marriage any

way we want, but we can't ignore its religious origins. From a historical standpoint, marriage has existed in accordance with religious dogmas and/or cultural
74

traditions that were used to preserve ones bloodline.

When we look back in time, we see that different cultures tell different stories of the symbolism of marriage, in accordance with the traditions of their culture. What we'll see that is similar is the incestuous factors involved. Rather it is the ancient Egyptian story of "Osiris" marrying his sister "Isis," or the biblical account of incest such as:

"Genesis 20:11-12 Abraham replied 'I said to myself there is surely no fear of God in this place, and they will kill me because of my wife. Besides she is also my sister, the daughter of my father though not of my mother; and she became my wife."

My point is very simple, from ancient times until now, marriage has always existed within the accepted mentality of the society in which one is getting married. Especially within those societies that recognizes its laws are of a religious foundation, therefore impacting what is socially acceptable or not. In today's time we will shun such incestuous acts, even if it's in the name of preserving ones bloodline.

The Islamic prophet Muhammad married the 9-year old daughter of one of his followers (Abu Bakre). In our society, we will prosecute him for child molestation. In their society, he is the "perfect example" for man to follow. Again, the acceptance of marriage simply depends on the society in question.

To legally ban gay marriage in America is the most hypocritical act this government can make. Not only is it against the very concept of liberty; it is a mockery of the ideal of democracy. And what of the separation of church and state? Even though the argument of the separation of church and state wasn't of constitutional origins, it was upheld in the courts.

Surely we can all agree that in our society, marriage is no longer solely a religious ritual. My Queen and I were married in the Bronx Supreme Court building. That fact is that the government should not have the right to say who should, or shouldn't get married. The pursuit of happiness can only be determined by those who are pursuing what makes them happy. Especially when their pursuit is in no way harming anyone else.

When we allow our government to dictate who can or cannot get married, then we are allowing our government to become a dictatorship, not a democracy. Marriage is a sacred vow between two individuals, symbolizing their desire to share the rest of their lives together as one. Who has the right to strip someone of such tranquility?

Proposition 8 changed part of the California states constitution, by restricting the states constitutions definition of marriage to mean:
"Only marriage between a man and woman is valid or recognized in the state of California."
(Section 7.5 article 1)

I thought that 'we the people' were the ones who determine what legislation is supposed to be passed on our behalf. Well, the campaign for gay marriage raised 43million dollars, and the polls had 56.4 percent of the people for the right of gay to be married. I don't get it. What makes the state government think that they are greater than the people?

These types of actions are the reason why the various groups need to join together. Rather we agree with particular issues on a personal level or not, what's 'right' is 'right.' If we are to stand for what is 'just,' we need to do it together. If we don't, then we all lose.

Chapter Ten

From Da' Hood to the Schools

Let us all understand this, America produces greatness. Slowly this greatness is becoming extinct. The principles that made America a world power, is loosing it value. When we stopped the "pledge of allegiance" in our public schools, we indirectly stripped our children of the concept of loyalty.

We are Americans, and as Americans we are obligated to pledge allegiance to the flag of the United States of America, because we are a republic. And we should instill in our children to be loyal to this republic, in which we stand, one nation, under God, indivisible, with liberty, and justice for all Americans. Our system of government is government of the people. If someone has an issue with their child being taught to pledge allegiance to this republic, then they should 'home school' their children. It's really that simple.

When we teach our children to say the 'pledge of allegiance' in school, they row up desiring to be a part of something greater then 'self.' We no longer allow our children to sing the 'star spangled banner' in schools. Our attempts to be 'politically correct' are making our children morally bankrupt. Why is the Puerto-Rican day parade (which is a beautiful event), a larger event in New York than the 'Independence day parade?' Did being 'politically correct' make us forget that 500 thousand patriots die to save the union, and free the slaves?

In California, 'Cinco de Mayo' (Spanish for the 5th of May), is a larger event than 'Independence day.' How lost have we become, that we will celebrate the independence of Mexico, but not of America? Did we forget what President Lincoln said in the Gettysburg address? Let me remind you:

"But, in a larger sense, we cannot dedicate-we cannot consecrate- we cannot hollow-this ground. The brave men, living and dead, who struggled here, have consecrated it far above our poor power to add or detract. The world will little note nor long remember what we say here, but it can never forget what they did here. It is for us, the living rather, to be dedicated here to the unfinished work which they who fought here have thus so nobly advanced. It is rather for us to be here dedicated to the great task remaining before us-that from these honored dead we take increased devotion to that cause for which they gave the last full measure of devotion; that we here highly resolve that these dead

shall not have died in vain; that this nation, under God, shall have a new birth of freedom; and that government of the people, by the people, for the people, shall not perish from the earth. "

It is our obligatory duty to keep the next generation conscious of the trails & tribulation that have been overcome, so that we now have the freedom to pursue what makes us happy. We must teach them of the obstacles that have been overcome so that we will have the equality to create our own opportunities for success; however we may define success to be. Politically correctness should be to tell those that come to America to prosper, that either they adapt to the politics of America, or go back home.

African Americans must understand that to continue to allow ourselves to be misled by false leaders, that are just out to make a name for themselves is stripping our children of self determination. The Democratic Party has purchased minorities. First with Lyndon b Johnson with his so-called "war on poverty," and fake concept of a "great society." And now Barack Obama, with his socialist ideology of redistribution of wealth, and "Obama care." We must stop accepting hand outs. Nobody owes us, but us.

Stop giving your pennies to 'Farrakhan's' to live in big mansions, with gold chandeliers while you're struggling to feed your children.

How come 85% of stores within the inner-city are owned by foreigners? I'll tell you why, we have allowed 'Sharptons' and 'Jackson's' to convince us that we are in need of programs like 'affirmative action.' We have allowed people like Luis Farrakhan, and the new black panthers to convince us that we need to take from the system to succeed. And yet, foreigners come to America understanding that the declaration of independence, the United States constitution, and the bill of rights guarantees that self determination provides equality in opportunity.

The equality to find a means to capitalize off of your ideas. The equality to reach your aspirations and the equality to create opportunities where there is none. But, when you have leaders that creates the perception of 'class wars,' and use racism to convince people they are stagnated because 'the system' is designed that way, then you're witnessing the true destruction of a black civilization.

I don't embrace stigmas that represent the ignorance of a people. I use the term "African American" only because it's the accepted term when referring to blacks. But, I identify myself as American. I was born in Harlem Hospital in New York City, and I must admit that it took me much adversity to understand that the life I was living was not only extremely self destructive, but also very un-American.

To live as an American is to live a life of high morality. To live as an American is to embrace patriotism and community awareness. To live as an American, is to have virtues, and to find pleasure in fighting for what is just. To live as an American is to believe in the United States constitution and fight for its preservation, and use it as the foundation for American standards.

My Queen and I were speaking about the lack of education of minorities, especially where race and nationality are concerned. I explained to her that she shouldn't allow herself to fall into that ignorant matrix that most Spanish people fall into, by calling herself "Latino." Yes, her parents are Puerto-Rican, but she is American (born in Cook County hospital in Chicago, Illinois). I explained that all these people calling themselves "Latin" are not "Latin."

When we go back, we will find that when ancient Rome was first bought down to its knees, (attacked from by the 'Huns' from the west, and the 'Franks' from the east), there was a small tribe that survived basically untouched. This tribe was known as "Latius." These are the people who had originally rebuilt the Roman Empire. Their language, as we know was (and still is) called 'Latin.' By the time that the muslims conquered and colonized these people, their language had already spread throughout Europe, due to the fact that they were a maritime civilization. The Spanish conquistadors spoke a broken dialect of their language, which is the Spanish that most people speak today. The reason that it's spoken so widely is because the conquistadors imposed it upon the people who they conquered for the papacy.

Whatever land the conquistadors colonized, they stamped as "Latin America," claiming the land as ownership of the Roman Catholic Church. 'Arawak,' 'Taino,' and 'Inca' Indian tribes that inhabited these lands eventually died off either by murder, famine, or eventually racially mixing with the African slaves. These people eventually accepted the title of 'Latino.'

82

My Queen researched and understood this. She realized that history is not the past…it is the manifestation of how we got to where we are today. It is a dead truth that gives living answers. In all the worlds recorded history, there has never been a government such as ours. I don't care what civilization one attempts to compare us to. There has never been a government on the face of this earth, like the United States government. Irving Brant, when speaking of the 'Bill of Rights,' stated:

"In all the worlds' history, there is nothing to compare with the pledges of human rifts and freedoms that have been worked into our charter of government…"

And this is known the world over. We Americans take our rights and freedoms for granted, and in doing so we are losing our traditions, as well as our identity. In the beginning of the building of the United States of America, there is a sad story. A story of the morbid enslavement of millions of people. A story of the murders of millions of innocent indigenous people.

But out of this great sorrow, arose a nation of glory. A nation of pride and a nation of unity. And because of this, we should reinstate the 'Pledge of Allegiance," in our public school system. And to all of our leaders that seem to want to instill in minorities, that 'the system' owes us something, let me remind you of the words of president Abraham Lincoln:

"And I hereby enjoin upon the people so declared to be free to abstain fro all violence, unless necessary in self defense; and I recommend to them that, in all cases where allowed, they labor faithfully for reasonable wages."

What this means, is that when our ancestors were emancipated, the door was now open for us to work for "reasonable wages" so that they (and eventually us) can provide for their families through self-determination. Self determination should be the foundation taught tour children. Not the concept of "redistribution of wealth." When President Kennedy said:

"If a free society cannot help the many who are poor, it cannot save the few who are rich…"

He was not speaking about the government coercing those with money to give it up with excessive taxation. That would be punishing people for being successful. He used the word 'help' to imply a willingness to assist. A choice. Lets stop demanding the 40 acres of land, and a damn 'mule' that we didn't work for, and probably wouldn't know what to do with.

Lets get it together.

Chapter Eleven

A letter to my Queen

My exotic Queen...

There is so much that I desire to say to you in this letter. But, I know that I must contain myself due to the publication of this work. However, some things that I have to say you should be shared with the world.

Let me begin...

Babygirl, from the day we've met you saw something in me that I didn't know I had. Passion and potential. The passion to make changes, not only in my life; but, also in the lives of others. You saw past the blood in my eyes, and the pain that dwelled within the deepest depths of my soul. You saw past the big brutish exterior,

and knew that there was more to me than the eyes tended to see. For whatever reason, you decided that you wanted to break through the barriers that I carefully built to protect my emotions from the cold indifference that the world has shown me. I thank you for that. I truly thank you…

In the beginning, you were disturbed by the way in which I dealt with people. You believed that my rudeness was counter-productive to my goals and dreams. You believed that the harsh brutality, in which I dealt with my associates, would eventually land me back in prison. But what scared you most was the fact that you thought that the way I disrespected my mother was a reflection on how I viewed woman in general. I've learned so much from your love, and guidance.

And I want to expound on a couple of those things…

First of all, I want to say that with the exception of how I deal with my mother, you were 100% correct about everything else. I don't have to be hostile towards people to get what I want. And if I do, I don't need to deal with those people. For how can I grow as an individual, if I'm constantly dealing with people who have no desire to grow? Stagnation will only bring about stagnation. Because of your love, I took three steps back and looked at the individuals that I was dealing with.

And this is what I saw…

Cowards! Drug dealers that have no heart, and used my potential for extreme violence to destroy our people with their irrational lust for ghetto glory. Slum lords that used my appearance to scare unsuspecting tenants into paying their rents, although living in unhealthy conditions. Club owners using my reputation to keep organized crime figures from extorting them, while they are having sex with under aged girls, and abusing others because they felt secure due to my protection.

Crooked Bronx politicians wanting to use me to reach the gangs in Da' Hood, so it'll look like they were doing something for the community, but only cared about re-election. Rappers that had "beef" calling me to roll with them to concerts, because they couldn't live up to all that gangster talk. So they wanted the 'silver-back' to show face for them. But when I fell in love for the first time in my life and told everyone that I was out of 'the game,' my phone stopped ringing.

You made me step back and look at my life. And what I've learned destroyed something in me...but it also made me want something greater. For the first time in my life, I went looking for a job. I knew that

it wouldn't be easy due to my criminal history, but I figured that I'll just go to one of the many people I know that owns big businesses. First I tried the big time Chinese millionaire David Louie. He told me that he can't give me a job because I'm "not Chinese." He didn't have a problem having drinks with me when I was protecting his son though.

And everyone else that I went to after that, it was the same story; or they offered me some 'dirty work.' But, I stood strong in my convictions to change my life. First for you, then eventually for me. Doing the right thing is hard...so very hard. But, love is greater than the adversity. So I continue to try.

This year makes seven years that you and I exist as one. It's been an experience that has been both wonderful, and sorrowful. But I wouldn't change it for anything in the world. I have found a heart within me that has been lying dormant for far too long. Because of you, I want to make a change not only in my life, but also in the lives of others.

You have awakened a sleeping giant. A good giant. A giant of compassion and understanding. A giant of self determination, and the will to inspire others to get up, and make a change in their lives. A giant that now knows that life is only fruitful when you contribute to the growth of society. You give life substance, and value. You make doing good worth the adversity that tends to come along with it.

I always knew deep in my heart, that something good would eventually come my way. I just never thought it would be in the form of something as exquisite, and exotic as you. Your love, and passion…your protectiveness and wisdom…your smile and innocence…your tenderness and tenaciousness, all create a woman of greatness. A woman that lights the darkest of nights, with a glow that illuminates the darkest of souls. Thank you for coming to me. Thank you for standing by me. Thank you for giving me the inspiration and drive to bring out my greatest potential. And for you, I will dedicate my life to the growth and development of inner-city minorities, so that they won't have to face the same adversity that has, at one time, blackened my soul.

There are times when we don't see eye to eye, it is at those times that I truly love you the most; though you might not see it, or I might not express it. But never forget that you are truly my soul mate. I am not capable of expressing my love for you in totality, my vocabulary is absolutely too limited for me to take on such a task. But if you look deep into my eyes…you will see all there is to know that I love you…and always will.

Yours truly,
Eldon.

Chapter Twelve

Taking the Initiative

"Don't you understand that we first begin by telling stories to children? And surely they are false on the whole, though they have some truth in them. And we use stories on children before physical training."
(Socrates; 'Plato Republic')

I remember when I first read this paragraph in the 'Republic.' I was lying down beside my wife reading into the wee hours of night, and when I read it, I woke my baby up to speak to her about it. Of course she was pissed off at being awakened at 3am to talk about the book that I was reading…but she loves me, so she gave in.

All throughout history, in every culture on the face of

this earth, oral teachings has been used to educate the youth. In ancient Egypt, it was the 'Memphite equation,' in ancient Greece, it was the stories of 'Zeus,' in Nordic mythology it was the stories of 'Odin,' and how the gods went to war with the giants and the gods sent thunderbolts at the giants, and these ice thunderbolts are responsible for creating the earth.

No matter what culture that we decide to speak about, we will always find 'common' oral traditions, with the exception of the United States of America.

Because America is a mass multi-cultural society, we have various oral traditions from every nation on the face of the earth. And this is one of the many reasons that there exist such a large hiatus amongst American citizens. With no common culture, and the constant elimination of American traditions we are depriving our youth of an identity.

I have a friend that I grew up with, named Anthony Wells. He denounced his American citizenship, and calls himself something 'Bey.' Now, he tells me that he changed his name to 'Bey' as a way of showing that he is "free of the slave-masters grasp.' He even went as far as to tell me that I should change my name to Eldon Bey. Even though I got a good laugh at that, it really wasn't funny. He doesn't seem to realize that if he is attempting to rid himself of a "slave name" he's not doing it by adopting the name 'Bey.' Let me explain....

Bey is a Semitic language. It is not of African origins, and Semitic people were the first to enslave Africans, as mentioned earlier in this book. Now, I will go a little deeper into the etymology of Semitic languages to bring forth a better understanding.

When we talk about Semitic languages, we have to remember that most Semitic languages survived due to religious texts, because most Semitic languages were used solely in spoken form due to the lack of formal education of the masses of Semitic people. Semitic languages are broken down into three categories; 1) eastern Semitic 2) western Semitic 3) and southern Semitic.

The east is considered the Mesopotamian region, the west is considered the Syrian (and later on Lebanon) region, and the south is considered the Arabian peninsular (and later on Ethiopian) region. Now, when we look at the origins of the name 'Bey,' this name (or title) is from Semitic people. The very first oppressors of African people.

Bey is of Turkish origins, and means 'chieftain.' Other Arab nations used the term as well. For example, the Persian leaders were called "Bay," "Baig," "Beigh," which means 'Lord.' Now, the Moorish science temple of America was started by Timothy Drew. A young Black American born in New Jersey that taught that black Americans were here before the slave trade and that their religion was another sect of Islam. He also claimed that Blacks are really 'Asiatic' (referring to the paleoamericans that's not considered Mongoloids), Mongoloids), and called themselves "Indigenous Moors." So, he's still a 'slave,' because he's using a different "slave masters name."

Not to mention that his so-called religion is nothing more than a big business. The Moorish Science Temple of America is registered with the Chicago department of state, under the Illinois act 805 ILCS 110.

However, like many other religions, or 'sects' that we tend to follow we need to research what we're getting into. We follow these so-called religions only as an attempt to be a part of 'something.' To belong… we're searching for an identity. And the more we worry about political correctness…the more we worry about offending the religious dogmas of other cultures, the more we take away from the American fundamentals, the more we will become lost in our search for self. The more our children will become gang bangers, and the more religious fanatics will easily find recruits.

We need to begin teaching our children American history at a very young age. In the process of teaching American history, they will learn world history because the root of American history begins outside of America. They would learn of different cultures, and religions. They would learn of different nationalities, and grow appreciating these differences, understanding that these differences are what make America great. But most importantly, they will have an identity.

Chapter Thirteen

Conclusion

I always wanted to be a writer. I never thought that I would write a book on this particular topic. Fortunately for me, many people believed that I possess a certain "rawness" that people need to hear. Maybe I do... maybe I don't. But what I do have is a lot to say about the conditions of our inner-city youth, and the unjust stereo-types that's placed upon them. The hardships that our youths face today, socially conditions them to be deviants. Life itself is dealing these children unfair hands to play from day one.

Parents in the ghetto have this mentality where when their children reach a certain age that they have to go out there and "get yours." The perfect example of this is a boy named 'Brian' that my wife and I deal with.

One day Brian came to our house on the verge of tears. When we asked what's wrong, he told us that he would like if I could talk to his father for him. He explained that Mike (his father) told him he had to drop out of school and work with him, because it was time for him to contribute to the house.

Now, Brian had just turned seventeen and really wanted to finish school. I eventually spoke to Mike, but the damage was already done. Brian hit the streets, and he ended up getting shot. I don't know what Brian doing at this time. But I know that he didn't finish school because his father was not a father. And I know that society views this kid as a menace. My wife and I know that he is (or was) a very good kid that wanted more out of life than St. Lawrence Avenue in the Bronx had to offer. That is an unjust hand.

Or take my little man Arron. Seventeen years old, in prison for second degree murder. He is a smart young man that lost his eldest brother to another youth's gun, and his younger brother to a drunken man's car. His father only loves him if he doesn't have to give him money, and even though his mother loves him, she has given up on trying to do something that she simply didn't know how to do…raise a child. She condemns his actions, and yet she had him doing things that jeopardized his freedom, and ultimately his life. He was dealt an unfair hand.

I can give numerous accounts of children that have been dealt these unfair hands. And its heart wrenching. And to make matters worst, society at large places stigmas on these children that they will eventually embrace, and act accordingly. And animal activist asked how come we're not involved in the struggle for animal rights... we're to much involved in the struggle to save our youth.

Our so-called leaders are busy calling Rush Limbaugh, Sean Hannity, and Mark Lavin racist for trying to tell people to stop depending on the government to provide for them, and get up and do for self. Why would you want your people to be dependant upon federal, state, and local government? Because it gives them power. Because as long as people possess the mentality that they are 'entitled' to tax payer dollars, these leaders have a job!

If you take away a persons belief in 'self,' and make them believe they need you to survive, you keep them enslaved...and you now hold the masters whip. They will march when you say March, and they will agitate when you say agitate. And while they continue to suffer, you line your pockets. These leaders are slave masters, and their followers are the slaves. They complain that there are no jobs, and yet they protest wall mart coming to New York. Such hypocrisy!

If we can spend 1.2 billion dollars a year in clothing, and 500 million a year in music, then collectively we're far from poor. We can do better when we do better together. It's not about race, color, or religion, these are tools that are used by those who desire to capitalize off of racism. It's about recognizing that we are the source of our problems. And once recognizing this, act accordingly.

Animal rights activist, I truly appreciate your desire

to have minorities involved in the struggle for animal rights, and animal liberation. But, I also have a question for you; do you want minorities involved because you believe it would give you more leverage...or do you want minorities involved because we have the heart to do the things most of you won't?

Chapter Fourteen

Food for Thought- Demonizing Who?

Are we that naive to believe that differences of opinions, is demonizing those whom we disagree with? That is what's happening with these hearings on the lack of American Muslim assistance in fighting Islamic extremist. I believe that there is nothing wrong with 'political correctness.' However, too much of anything is not good. And where religion is concerned, political correctness is being used as a weapon to keep people quiet; and where Islam is concerned, we are at the point of showing outright fear of the religion.

Lets understand that Muslims do possess a separatist mentality when in comes to non-Muslims. You can walk into any masjid in New York, and feel the animosity and skepticism that Muslims have towards non-Muslims. You can ask any Muslims in New York for assistance, and you will find that they will hesitate to help you if you're not Muslim.

Now, I do understand that Muslims, like any other group in America is comfortable being around people that they have something in common with. That is human nature. However, because American culture is multi-culturalism, Muslims like any other religious organization must learn to assimilate. Especially, if they desire to live in harmony with other religions or ethnicities.

Since the 911 terrorist attacks, America has been on guard when it comes to terrorism. And with the many failed attempts of American Muslims to cause havoc on American soil, people are justified in having fear of Muslims. Now before I continue, let me clearly state that I have absolutely no animosity against Muslims. Personally, I believe that Islam is a beautiful religion if followed in accordance with the Quran. Unfortunately, I personally don't know any Muslims that do so.

If we were to analyze the main principles of Islam, which is known as "The Five Pillars of Islam," we would see a code of ethics that truly benefits the growth of any society. They are as follows:

- 1) Shahada (creed)
- 2) Salat (daily prayer)
- 3) Sawm (fasting)
- 4) Zakat (charity)
- 5) Hajj (pilgrimage)

Shahada is an Arabic word, literally meaning; "to witness." In Islam, Shahada is the main principle that an individual must embrace to become Muslim. It is stating that an individual acknowledges that there is no God but Allah, and Muhammad is his messenger. This is an oath taken by all Muslims, and the beauty of acknowledging that there exists a higher power can not be understated.

Sawm is an Arabic word for fasting. However it goes much deeper than simply abstaining from food, and water. In accordance with Islamic jurisprudence, Sawm includes abstaining from anything that is against Islamic law on the holy month of Ramadan. Fasting is considered a pious act in Islam. It is showing gratitude for Allah, and also benefits the mind and body by developing self-discipline, and cleansing the body.

Salat is Arabic for prayer. Muslims are prescribed to pray five times a day. Dawn (fajr), Noon (thuhr), Late noon (Asr), Sunset (maghrib), and Nightfall (isha'). This act of consistent prayers, are to always remain conscious of Gods grace.

Zakat is Arabic for charity. It is obligatory for all Muslims to give to charity. In the Sunni sect of Islam, Muslims are required to give 2.5% of their yearly income to charity.

Hajj is Arabic for pilgrimage. It is required by all Muslims to take a trip to the holy city of Mecca (if possible), atleast once in their lifetime.

Theses five principles of Islam are a great way to show

praise to ones God. Such mellifluous principles, instills humbleness and appreciation for life, within all who embraces these concepts. So what seems to be the problem? The problem is called idealism. Religious leaders tend to develop these believes that there way of seeing things are the right way, and begin manipulating their followers to embrace their ideals of creating a utopia based on their interpretation of what the religious books mean. These leaders tend to be radical, and therefore instill extreme measures within their followers to accomplish their goals of dominance.

We all have witnessed the disastrous results of the actions of these leaders. When people seek guidance, they will tend to follow anything that sounds good. We see that on a daily basis in the Black community. The built up frustration of joblessness, hunger, and drug addiction tends to make us follow any leader who claims to have the solutions to our problems.

This is the same thing that takes place within Muslim circles. And just like Black Americans, Muslims tend to only embrace other Muslims because they are indoctrinated to believe that no one else understands their adversity, therefore there is no need to assimilate with American society. This is very dangerous, because it breeds extreme animosity, and stereo-types towards Muslims.

Muslims are the only ones that can stop this animosity from continuing, by working with authorities in combating Islamic extremist, and working with grassroots community organizations in their struggle against self-afflicting genocide.

American Muslims must understand that non-Muslim people do not understand their religion, or the principles that Islam is supposed to stand on. We judge in accordance to what we see in the media, and usually that is NOT good. If Muslims become involved with the growth & development of the communities in which they reside, then we will see that the stereo-types of all Muslims being extremist will eventually cease.

However, we are not "Demonizing" anyone, by questioning the role played by American Muslims in combating Muslim terrorist. If anything Muslims are "Demonizing" us by declaring war on innocent people and attempting to murder as many innocent Americans as possible, and justifying their actions using religious dogma.

And yet, we hide from this reality by using the term "political correctness." Political correctness, is putting American lives in danger. And this needs to stop. We must face our opposition, and address the issues that are affecting the lives of our people, and act accordingly. We are so worried about how the world sees us, that we forgot how to look at ourselves. What we tend to forget is that America doesn't have to wonder how we look in the eyes of other nations, because the people of other nations are flooding our borders, trying to come here. That's all the answers that we need.